THE SCIENCE BEHIND NATURAL DISASTERS

TORNADOES

THE SCIENCE BEHIND TERRIBLE TWISTERS

Dr. Alvin Silverstein, Virginia Silverstein
and Laura Silverstein Nunn

Enslow Publishers, Inc.

40 Industrial Road
Box 398
Berkeley Heights, NJ 07922
USA

http://www.enslow.com

Library of Congress Cataloging-in-Publication Data

Silverstein, Alvin.
  Tornadoes: the science behind terrible twisters / Alvin Silverstein, Virginia Silverstein, and Laura Silverstein Nunn.
      p. cm.—(The science behind natural disasters)
  Includes bibliographical references and index.
  Summary: "Discusses the science behind tornadoes, including how and where they form, the scientific methods to track and predict them, and tornado safety tips"—Provided by publisher.
  ISBN-13: 978-0-7660-2976-7
  ISBN-10: 0-7660-2976-X
  1. Tornadoes—Juvenile literature. I. Silverstein, Virginia B. II. Nunn, Laura Silverstein. III. Title.
  QC955.2.S55 2009
  551.55'3—dc22
                    2008029635

Printed in the United States of America

10 9 8 7 6 5 4 3 2 1

To Our Readers: We have done our best to make sure all Internet Addresses in this book were active and appropriate when we went to press. However, the author and the publisher have no control over and assume no liability for the material available on those Internet sites or on other Web sites they may link to. Any comments or suggestions can be sent by e-mail to comments@enslow.com or to the address on the back cover.

Enslow Publishers, Inc., is committed to printing our books on recycled paper. The paper in every book contains 10% to 30% post-consumer waste (PCW). The cover board on the outside of each book contains 100% PCW. Our goal is to do our part to help young people and the environment too!

Illustration Credits: AP/Wide World Photos, pp. 1, 24, 26, 30, 40; Dave Kaup/ Reuters, p. 6; Enslow Publishers, Inc., p. 20; © Copyright 2005 Eric Nguyen, p. 18; © Copyright 2006 Eric Nguyen, p. 10; Gary Hincks/Photo Researchers, Inc., p. 23; © Gene & Karen Phoden/Visuals Unlimited, p. 36; Illustration by John M. Evans, USGS, Colorado District, p. 12; Jaime Oppenheimer/ MCT/ Landov, p. 7; Jim Reed/Photo Researchers, Inc., p. 34; Michael W. Skrepnick, p. 15; © Nancy P. Alexander/Visuals Unlimited, p. 38; NOAA Photo Library/ OAR/ ERL/ National Severe Storms Laboratory (NSSL), pp. 4, 22, 33; Photo by Bob McMillan/FEMA News Photo, p. 39; Reuters/ Jim Young/ Landov, p. 8.

Cover Illustration: Alan R. Moller/ Getty Images.

CONTENTS

In 2007, people living in Greensburg, Kansas, found out just how powerful a tornado could be—the twisting winds whipped through the small town, destroying nearly everything in the storm's path.

The monster tornado in Greensburg, Kansas, started out as a violent thunderstorm that developed in Texas on May 4, 2007, around 5 P.M. The storm strengthened as it moved northeast through

A tornado is formed when a funnel cloud reaches the ground. The cloud may be narrow or very wide.

Does Kansas Have More Tornadoes Than Anywhere Else?

Thanks to *The Wizard of Oz* film, many people think of Kansas when they think of tornadoes. Most of the world's tornadoes do occur in the central part of the United States. But Kansas is not the Number 1 hotspot for tornadoes. More tornadoes hit Texas and Oklahoma on average every year than anywhere else on Earth.

The high school in Greensburg, Kansas, was one of the many buildings in the town that was destroyed.

Oklahoma and then to Kansas. At about 8:30 P.M., storm chasers (people who drive around looking for severe storms and tornadoes) spotted a funnel-shaped cloud forming in Clark County, southwest of Greensburg. They reported this to the National Weather Service, which sent out tornado warnings for the area. The funnel cloud was moving across the county at about 32.2 kilometers (20 miles) per hour.[1]

By 9:30 P.M. it seemed certain that a tornado was going to hit at Greensburg. Storm chasers reported that the tornado was huge—at least 1.6 kilometers (1 mile) wide. The National Weather Service issued a tornado warning, and sirens went off in the town. People in Greensburg hurried into basements—

their own, or those of neighbors, and of community centers, such as schools, churches, and libraries.

About 10 P.M., the tornado touched down at Greensburg and swept through the town. Its powerful winds ripped trees out of the ground and ripped apart houses, businesses, and other buildings. The National Weather Service later reported that the funnel cloud was 2.7 kilometers (1.7 miles) wide and left a trail of destruction 35.2 kilometers (22 miles) long. Its winds blew at amazing speeds—at least 330 kilometers (205 miles) per hour.[2]

In just twenty minutes, the tornado had destroyed nearly

The tornado leveled most of the buildings in Greensburg, Kansas.

Residents clean up tornado damage in Greensburg, Kansas, on May 9, 2007.

95 percent of the town.[3] Most of the houses and all of the churches, schools, and businesses on Main Street were gone. Scott Reinecke, a Greensburg resident, described the scene: "It's incredible . . . you could hear things banging around, wood breaking . . . We had someone's furnace in our living room. I'm having difficulty recognizing my own town."[4]

Most of the town's fifteen hundred residents were able to get to shelters before the tornado hit.[5] But ten people in Greensburg died in the storm. Considering all the destruction, officials were amazed that there were not more deaths.[6] Although the townspeople had only about twenty minutes to prepare, the warning was enough time to save many lives.

Lost and Found

After the storm, the prize exhibit at the Greensburg town museum—a 454-kilogram (1,000-pound) meteorite, insured for one million dollars—was missing. People thought the tornado had blown it away. A few days later, however, a museum volunteer dug out the missing meteorite from the rubble at the museum site.

WHAT'S THE WEATHER?

Every day, people all over the world make plans based on the weather. But sometimes, weather conditions change unexpectedly. Bright, sunny skies may turn dark and stormy. And if the conditions are right, a tornado may develop.

All weather, whether it is calm or stormy, occurs in Earth's atmosphere. The atmosphere is a mixture of gases that blankets our planet. The weather is constantly changing because the atmosphere is constantly changing. Extreme weather conditions, such as tornadoes, are the result of major changes in the atmosphere.

These large hailstones fell in Texas during a thunderstorm.

11

Something in the Air

The atmosphere contains moisture, in the form of a gas called water vapor. The water vapor in the air comes mostly from the surface of oceans through a process called the water cycle. Sunlight heats up the oceans, causing large amounts of water to evaporate, or change from a liquid to a gas. The warm, moist air rises into the atmosphere. As winds carry the moist air away, it begins to cool. Eventually the water may cool down enough to

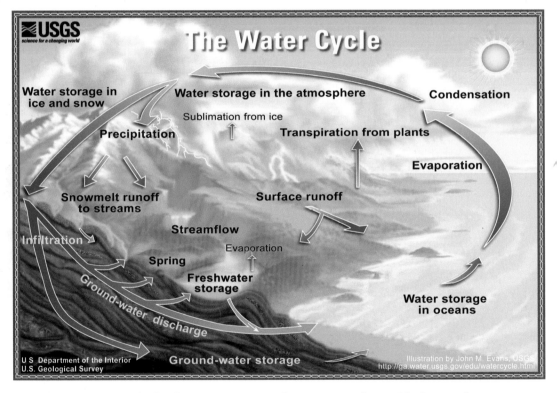

The water cycle is the movement of water on, in, and above the Earth. Earth's water is always changing states, from liquid to vapor to ice and back again. The water cycle has been working for billions of years, and all life on Earth depends on it.

condense, turning into tiny water droplets or freezing as ice crystals. These make up clouds, mist, and fog. When the droplets or crystals become too heavy to stay up in the air, the clouds return water back to Earth's surface as precipitation—rain, snow, sleet, or hail. This completes the water cycle.

Air on the Move

The air is made up of gas molecules, particles far too small to see without a very good microscope. The molecules in cold air move very slowly and are very close together. This makes them heavier than warm-air molecules, and they sink toward the ground. As gas molecules get heated, they move faster. The moving molecules bang into each other, forcing them to take up more room than when they were colder. When colder air sinks, it takes the place of warmer air and pushes the warmer air higher. Thus, warm air rises and cool air falls.

Energy from the sun keeps the air molecules in constant motion. As warm air rises and cool air sinks, the atmosphere swirls and bubbles like water heating in a pot on the stove. Warm and cold air masses chase one another around the planet, producing winds. The moving air helps to spread the heat of the sunlight to parts of the world that are not heated directly. Moving air also spreads colder air to warm regions.

When only one air mass is moving over an area, the weather

is usually fair and stable. But two air masses may crash into each other and create stormy weather.

Under Pressure

You probably do not feel it, but air is constantly pressing down on you with tremendous force. This is called air pressure. Air pressure is the weight of all the air molecules above you.

Air pressure is an important factor in weather. You may have heard weather forecasters talk about "high-pressure systems" or "low-pressure systems." In high-pressure systems, winds blow from high up in the atmosphere down toward Earth's surface. Air becomes drier as it falls, so the weather becomes stable and fair.

Low-pressure systems are more unstable. Air pressure tends to push air from high-pressure areas to low-pressure areas. As the cold air sinks, warm air currents rise up into the sky in a swirling motion, forming clouds along the way. When the two air pressure systems meet, thunderstorms

Why Do Your Ears Pop?

Do your ears ever "pop" when you ride up in an airplane or high-rise elevator? That happens because there is a change in air pressure. As you go up, there are less gas molecules above your head in the atmosphere and the air pressure is lower. The air trapped inside your ears is at a higher pressure than the air outside your body. So your eardrums bulge to balance out the pressures, making a popping sound.

Thunderstorms start when warm, wet air rises high into the sky.

or other storm systems may occur. Tornadoes are produced by low-pressure systems.

Thunderstorms

Thunderstorms occur worldwide as many as 16 million times each year. In the United States, an estimated 100,000 thunderstorms develop each year. About 10 percent of them are considered severe.[1] According to the National Weather Service, a severe thunderstorm is one that produces a tornado, winds of at least 93 kilometers (58 miles) per hour, and/or hail 1.9 centimeters (¾ inch) in diameter or larger.

In North America, most thunderstorms take place in the spring and summer. Tall, puffy clouds called cumulonimbus are clues that a thunderstorm is coming. Thunderclouds need a lot

Why Do Storm Clouds Look Dark and Gray?

Clouds are made up of millions of tiny water droplets, packed close together. On a bright, sunny day, clouds look white because water droplets near the surface reflect sunlight. A thundercloud looks dark and gray because the tiny water droplets have joined to form larger ones. These droplets absorb some of the sun's rays that pass into the cloud. The storm cloud is so thick and heavy with moisture that little or no sunlight can pass through. A storm cloud off in the distance may look white, though, as sunlight reflects off its edge.

of moisture and heat to form, which is why they usually occur during warm weather. During hot, humid weather, thunderclouds may be very tall, sometimes reaching a height of more than 18 kilometers (11 miles). At that height, the temperatures are below freezing.

Hailstones sometimes fall during thunderstorms. The air currents in a thundercloud rise and fall constantly. As water droplets are carried up into the freezing temperatures at great heights, they freeze into tiny ice crystals. The ice particles collect more and more cloud droplets that freeze when they hit the ice. Layers of ice are added to the frozen particle, producing a larger and larger ball of ice—a hailstone. Eventually the hailstone gets so heavy that it falls to the ground. Most hailstones are about the size of a pea, but some are as big as softballs. Large hailstones can destroy crops, break windows, dent cars, and injure people.

UNDERSTANDING TORNADOES

The United States has an average of one thousand tornadoes every year—more than any other nation.[1] Any one of the fifty states is at risk for tornadoes, but most tornadoes actually develop in the central states. That is why people call this high-risk region Tornado Alley. Tornadoes are also common in Florida because thunderstorms occur often there. (Hurricanes can also produce both thunderstorms and tornadoes.) But the tornadoes in Florida are usually weaker than those

A type of storm called a supercell can quickly turn into a tornado.

in Tornado Alley. The term *tornado* comes from the Spanish word *tronada*, which means "thunderstorm." *Tronada* is derived from the Spanish verb *tornar*, meaning "to turn."

Tornadoes, or "twisters," are funnel-shaped storms with winds that swirl around rapidly like a spinning top. Tornadoes can drop from the bottoms of big thunderstorm clouds. But some tornadoes start close to the ground and rise up into a storm.

Compared to a hurricane, tornadoes are not very large storms. They are typically 130 to 170 meters (400 to 500 feet) wide, whereas a hurricane can cover hundreds of kilometers. Tornadoes may not be big storms, but they can produce the most powerful winds on Earth.

In Tornado Alley, most tornadoes form during spring

and summer. That is when thunderstorms occur most often. Tornadoes develop inside severe thunderstorms. Thousands of thunderstorms occur in the United States every year, but only a small number of them will produce tornadoes.

How Does a Tornado Form?

Tornadoes usually form when the weather is warm and humid. They can occur at any time of the day or night, but most of them develop between 3 and 9 P.M. By then, the sun has had time to heat up the ground and the air close to it. A layer of warm, moist air is trapped beneath the cold, dry air higher in the atmosphere.

As the cold air sinks, the warm, moist air near the ground rises, producing a strong updraft (upward-moving air). This updraft creates an area of low air pressure near the ground. Air from the surrounding area replaces the rising air. The rising air cools, and moisture condenses into water droplets. Huge thunderclouds build up in the sky. The cold, moist air in the clouds is heavier and moves downward. This is called a downdraft.

Does Tornado Alley Get Hurricanes Too?

Tornadoes and hurricanes are both types of cyclones— powerful windstorms that spin in a circle. But a hurricane is a *tropical* cyclone. It forms over warm, tropical waters. So the central part of the United States does not usually get hurricanes. (Texas is an exception—it gets tornadoes and also hurricanes that move in from the Gulf of Mexico.)

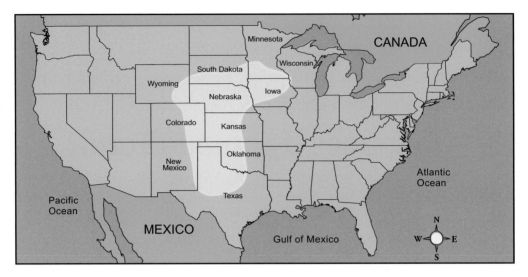

Tornado Alley (in yellow) is the part of the United States that has the most tornadoes. The most violent tornadoes also occur there.

Winds higher in the atmosphere blow faster and they may change direction. These changes in speed and direction as the winds move upward are called wind shear. The faster winds collide with the slower winds, and the air trapped between them starts to spin. At first the spinning effect is invisible. The condensing moisture releases heat, causing the updrafts to rise faster. Soon the whole thundercloud begins to rotate. It forms a severe type of thunderstorm called a supercell. Supercells are the storms most likely to produce tornadoes.

A spinning column of air called a vortex forms within the supercell. The vortex spins slowly at first, but it picks up speed as it sucks in more warm air. The storm grows larger and more powerful. The vortex spins faster and grows longer, hanging down from the bottom of the cloud. Now it looks like a funnel, and it is called a funnel cloud. This funnel of spinning air drops from the storm cloud until its tip touches the ground. When it touches down, it has become a tornado.

Touchdown!

The winds inside a funnel cloud are constantly spinning upward. The air below the funnel cloud is sucked up into the low-pressure area at the center. When the bottom of the tornado touches the ground, it will suck up objects in its path. Like a vacuum cleaner, it pulls up dust and dirt, and the swirling funnel cloud darkens. The powerful winds can sometimes lift large trees out of the ground and smash buildings into little pieces. Soon these objects whirl around inside the tornado and are eventually thrown back to the ground.

A tornado normally stays on the ground for no more than twenty minutes, although it can last up to three hours. But it does

Why Is Tornado Alley Such a Target?

Remember that storms develop when masses of warm and cold air crash into each other. This happens often in the Tornado Alley states. In the spring, strong, dry winds blow east from the Rocky Mountains across the plains. This draws warm, moist air north from the Gulf of Mexico. At the same time, cold, dry winds blow south from Canada. These warm and cold air masses collide. On the flat lands of Tornado Alley, there are no tall mountains to get in the way of the mixing air masses. Soon, big, swirling thunderstorms develop. Some of them turn into violent tornadoes.

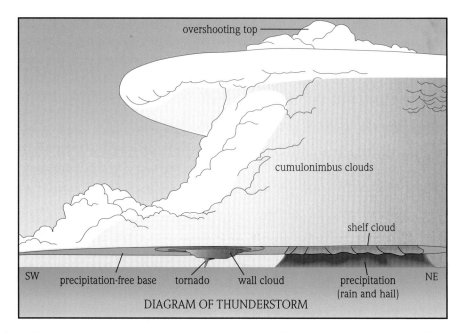

overshooting top

cumulonimbus clouds

shelf cloud

SW   precipitation-free base   tornado   wall cloud   precipitation   NE
(rain and hail)

DIAGRAM OF THUNDERSTORM

The clouds of a thunderstorm are very tall. Rain and hail usually fall on the northeast side of a storm. A tornado usually forms from a wall cloud on the southwest side of a storm.

not need much time to cause a lot of damage. Remember, a violent tornado destroyed most of Greensburg, Kansas, in just twenty minutes.

Tornadoes move over land at a speed of 30 to 90 kilometers (20 to 50 miles) per hour. In North America, tornadoes usually travel southwest to northeast. But they can move in any direction.

Tornadoes need warm, moist air to keep moving. When it starts to rain, cooler air sinks, pushing the rising warm air away from the thunderstorm. So the tornado's energy supply gets cut off. As it loses energy, the funnel cloud tilts and turns into a thin, ropy shape. Then it breaks up and disappears.

Sometimes a tornado's funnel cloud may rise, travel for awhile, and then touch down again in a different area. A thunderstorm can produce more than one tornado. In fact, two or more funnel clouds may drop down from the same storm cloud at the same time. Two tornadoes may travel along together, leaving two paths of destruction.

A number of tornadoes may hit the same area within a day or so. This area may be small, or it may extend over several states in the path of a moving storm system. Weather experts call a group of six or more tornadoes in the same region a tornado outbreak. The biggest outbreak on record was a series of 148 tornadoes that hit the United States and Canada on April 3 and April 4, 1974.

The arrows in this diagram show the direction of the tornado's movement and rotation.

WHEN A TORNADO HITS

4

Tornadoes have been recorded in every state of the United States, and on every continent except Antarctica. But many tornadoes do not get reported because they happen in wide-open spaces. Few people live in these places, and a tornado does not cause much damage where there are few buildings.

Many people live in Tornado Alley and other tornado hotspots, such as Florida. So when a tornado

Why Do Tornadoes Seem to Target Mobile Homes?

Tornadoes do not really target mobile homes. Mobile home communities seem to suffer the worst damage because the structures are lightweight and not well-anchored to the ground.

Tornadoes are very unpredictable. Sometimes, they destroy some houses while leaving others nearby completely intact. This was the case in Suffolk, Virginia, on April 29, 2008.

hits these areas, the effects can be disastrous. On average, tornadoes cause about eighty deaths a year in the United States, and more than fifteen hundred injuries.[1]

Whirling Winds

Tornado winds are extremely powerful. They can blow up to 483 kilometers (300 miles) per hour. However, about 98 percent of the tornadoes in the United States are not that severe.[2] In fact, their wind speeds are usually less than 241 kilometers (150 miles) per hour. But even these weaker storms can cause tremendous damage.

Tornadoes sometimes uproot trees. A tornado in Cammack Village, Arkansas, ripped this tree in a park from the ground in April 2008.

Strong gusts of wind can rip huge trees out of the ground. They can pick up cars and then throw them hundreds of feet away. A whole house can be smashed to pieces in a matter of seconds. These pieces are called debris. Actually, most of the injuries and deaths from tornadoes are caused by debris flying through the air. Even small objects, such as a piece of glass or metal, can be dangerous when they fly through the air at high speeds. People can be hurt or killed by this flying debris.

What is a Waterspout?

A waterspout is a tornado that moves over oceans, seas, or lakes. Waterspouts are typically weaker than tornadoes that form over land. But the winds of waterspouts are strong enough to be dangerous for boats, planes, and swimmers. They may also move onto land and damage areas along the shore.

Waterspouts are common in the waters around Florida. As many as five hundred occur each year in the Florida Keys.[3]

What's the Damage?

Scientists use a special rating scale to classify tornadoes. Theodore Fujita, a researcher at the University of Chicago, originally developed the scale in 1971. The Fujita (F) Scale rated the strength of tornadoes according to the damage they caused. It used damage reports to estimate the wind speeds.

A new system, called the Enhanced Fujita (EF) Scale,

THE ENHANCED FUJITA (EF) SCALE

CATEGORY	WIND SPEED	DAMAGES
EF0	105–137 km/hr (65–85 mph)	*Light damage:* • Some damage to chimneys • Branches broken from trees • Some damage to gutters or siding
EF1	138–178 km/hr (86–110 mph)	*Moderate damage:* • Mobile homes moved off foundation • Some trees blown down • Damage to roof shingles, doors, and windows • Moving cars blown off road
EF2	179–218 km/hr (111–135 mph)	*Considerable damage:* • Roofs ripped off frame houses • Mobile homes destroyed • Boxcars blown over • Large trees snapped or uprooted • Cars lifted into the air • Light objects become missiles
EF3	219–266 km/hr (136–165 mph)	*Severe damage:* • Roofs and some walls ripped off houses • Trains blown over • Most trees in wooded areas uprooted • Large cars lifted and thrown through the air
EF4	267–322 km/hr (166–200 mph)	*Devastating damage:* • Well-constructed houses destroyed • Structures with weak foundations blown away • Cars thrown a great distance • Large objects become missiles
EF5	> 322 km/hr (> 200 mph)	*Incredible damage:* • Strong frame houses destroyed and blown away • Structural damage to high-rise buildings • All trees and shrubs blown down or uprooted • Car-sized objects become missiles reaching long distances.

replaced the Fujita Scale in February 2007. Like the older system, the EF scale rates a tornado according to six categories, from EF0 (least powerful) to EF5 (most destructive). It gives more accurate estimates of wind speed, based on types of damage. It also classifies tornadoes according

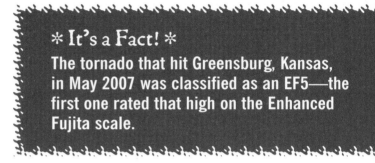

☀ It's a Fact! ☀
The tornado that hit Greensburg, Kansas, in May 2007 was classified as an EF5—the first one rated that high on the Enhanced Fujita scale.

to damage to twenty-eight different types of structures, including trees, mobile homes, barns, framed houses, strip malls, stores, and high-rise buildings.

Tornadoes can be very unpredictable. They may destroy the houses on one side of a street while leaving those on the other side untouched. Tornadoes also have been known to lift objects into the air and then set them down without a scratch. They can even lift a house off its foundation and set it down in another area.

TRACKING TORNADOES

Hurricanes can take days to form until they finally reach land. So there is plenty of time to warn people. But tornadoes are a different story. The thunderstorms that form tornadoes develop very quickly. The twenty-minute warning that the National Weather Service issued for Greensburg, Kansas, was actually longer than the usual time for a tornado warning. The average tornado warning gives people in the target area only 13 minutes to seek shelter.[1]

Weather scientists called meteorologists keep trying to improve their ability to predict tornadoes. Using technology, they track storm systems and look for signs that tornadoes might be forming.

A huge tornado touches down in Orchard, Iowa, on June 10, 2008.

Doppler Radar

Meteorologists use Doppler radar to collect information about clouds and precipitation. Doppler radar sends out radio waves from a big antenna. These radio waves bounce off raindrops and hailstones inside the clouds. The way these waves bounce shows the size and location of the storm clouds. Radar images are pieced together and viewed like a movie to track where the weather systems are moving. Doppler radar can also detect rotating winds in the clouds, typical of supercells, providing clues that a tornado might form. In fact, meteorologists often use this information to send out tornado watches.

Storm Spotters

Despite all the weather technology, probably the most important information for tracking thunderstorms and tornadoes comes from "storm spotters." Storm spotters are volunteers who are specially trained to watch for storm clouds and signs of tornadoes.

They belong to SKYWARN™, an organization created by the National Weather Service. SKYWARN™ has nearly 280,000 storm spotters all over the United States.[2]

When severe weather is expected, storm spotters keep a watchful eye on weather conditions in their local area. They look for developing storm clouds, rain, hail, and possible development of tornadoes. Sometimes they see weather conditions that have not been picked up by satellites or radar. Storm spotters immediately report the information to the National Weather

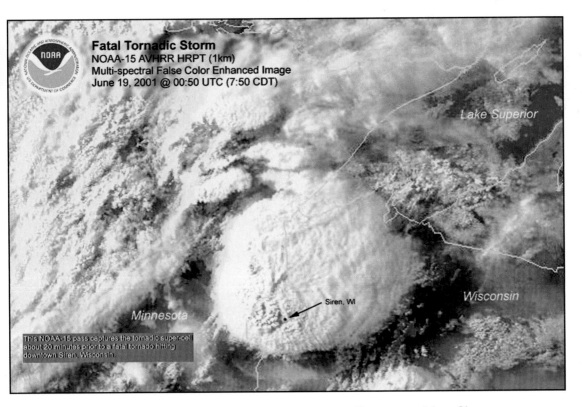

Fatal Tornadic Storm
NOAA-15 AVHRR HRPT (1km)
Multi-spectral False Color Enhanced Image
June 19, 2001 @ 00:50 UTC (7:50 CDT)

Lake Superior

Siren, WI

Wisconsin

Minnesota

This NOAA-15 pass captures the tornadic super-cell about 20 minutes prior to a fatal tornado hitting downtown Siren, Wisconsin.

This image from the NOAA shows a supercell approaching Siren, Wisconsin. Twenty minutes after this image was taken, the supercell produced a deadly tornado.

Storm Spotters or Storm Chasers?

The National Weather Service specially trains storm spotters. They report local weather conditions to the National Weather Service. Storm chasers travel all over the country following storms. Some storm spotters are also storm chasers. But many storm chasers do not have special training.

Professional storm chaser Katherine Bay takes a picture of a tornado in Turner County, South Dakota, during an outbreak of twisters on June 24, 2003.

Service. These firsthand reports give early warnings and may save many lives.

Storm Chasers

Storm chasers are experienced volunteers who drive around high-risk tornado areas, looking for tornadoes. They keep track of weather reports and drive to areas where storms have been spotted. Sometimes they cover hundreds of miles and cross several states in a single day. Many storm chasers drive vehicles carrying special equipment, such as satellite dishes that receive live information from weather stations. Portable tracking systems also help them find the areas where the storms have been reported.

Why do storm chasers chase storms? They may be meteorologists doing research and reporting information. Reporters, filmmakers, college students, and thrill-seekers may also chase tornadoes. Some storm chasers make money by taking people on storm-chasing "safaris."

Chasing tornadoes is very dangerous. Storm chasers try to stay a safe distance from the storm. But twisters change direction unexpectedly. They can also throw objects over great distances. Tornadoes have killed storm chasers. An untrained person should never try storm chasing. In fact, people in a tornado's path should seek shelter right away.

Storm Chaser Spotlight

On a stormy night in Manchester, South Dakota, in late June 2003, a huge tornado was just about to hit. The townspeople had run to tornado shelters. But Tim Samaras, a professional storm chaser, was parked on the road right in the tornado's path. When the twister was just 90 meters (100 yards) away, Samaras dropped a probe by the side of the road and then jumped into his van. He drove away only eighty seconds before the tornado reached that area where he had been.

Samaras's van was equipped with high-tech equipment, including radios, scanners, monitors, satellite tracking devices, and a wireless Internet connection. The probe he dropped off measured humidity, temperature, pressure, and wind speed and direction. It recorded the biggest pressure drop ever measured in a tornado. "This is a historic occasion," Samaras said. "But we were definitely too close."[3]

STAYING SAFE

If the National Weather Service issues a tornado warning just fifteen minutes before touchdown, can people really find safety? Yes. That may not sound like much time, but there are many things people can do to stay safe during a tornado. Being prepared is the key.

Emergency Plan

If a tornado hits, would you know what to do? First, you and your family need an emergency plan. Are there special storm shelters nearby?

Warning Signs

Sometimes tornadoes develop so quickly that there is no time for an official warning. But there are some warning signs that a tornado could be coming. These may include thunder and lightning; a dark, often greenish sky; large hailstones; or a loud roaring sound, much like that of a train.

Dust and debris fly as a strong tornado churns across the land near Manshester, South Dakota on Jun 24, 2003. This storm was part of the largest single-day outbreak of twisters in the state's history.

Tornado shelters are often built underground.

They are usually in the basements of community buildings, such as schools, churches, and libraries. Basements are good shelters because they are underground. You should know where your town's shelters are and the fastest way to get to them. Listen for tornado warnings on the radio or TV, and follow the instructions. If the local officials say to find a safe shelter, do not waste time. Leave as quickly as you can.

If there is not enough time to get to a town shelter and your house has a basement or cellar, stay there during a tornado. The high winds make it dangerous to go outside. A mobile home is a very unsafe place to be during a tornado, however. This kind of home is not sturdy and does not usually have a basement. People in mobile homes should leave and find a sturdy building nearby or a storm shelter.

At home, keep a disaster supply kit handy. You will need items to keep you safe in case the power goes out. Emergency supplies can get you through a few days stuck in your home or a shelter, until regular services are working again. The kit should include:

- Flashlight and batteries
- Battery-operated radio
- First aid kit
- Canned food and nonelectric can opener

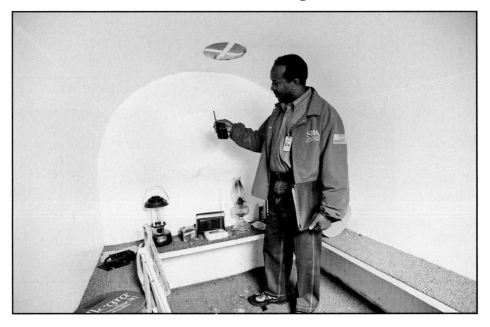

This underground storm shelter that was successfully used during a May 8, 2003 tornado that tore through Moore, Oklahoma.

- Bottled water
- Special items for babies, the elderly, and pets
- Protective clothing and shoes
- Blankets

When a Tornado Touches Down

Many towns in Tornado Alley have special sirens that sound when a tornado warning is issued. People living in these areas usually know what to do to keep their families safe. If you are caught in a tornado, follow these basic tips:

- Find shelter immediately. It should be a basement or an interior room (such as a closet or bathroom) on the lowest floor of a building. Bathtubs give good protection. Try to get under a heavy piece of furniture.
- Stay away from windows.

Amber Harrison works with a rescued dog at a makeshift shelter in Greensburg, Kansas, on May 7, 2007, after a massive EF5 tornado hit the town.

- If you are in a car, do not try to drive away from the tornado. Get out of the car and find a sturdy shelter.
- If you are outside and cannot find a shelter, lie flat in a ditch or on the ground. This will help protect you from flying debris, but it will not keep a tornado from lifting you into its funnel cloud.
- Be careful of flying debris. Cover your head with your hands.

Should You Keep Windows Open During a Tornado?

Some people think that keeping windows closed during a tornado will cause the house to explode. This is not true. Even though there is a huge drop in air pressure inside a tornado, it is not likely to make a whole house explode. In fact, opening windows during a tornado might actually cause *more* damage to a house.

- Do not seek shelter under a bridge or highway overpass. You may be hit by flying debris. Also, winds get stronger when they go under an overpass.

Scientists still have a lot to learn about tornadoes. We cannot stop these powerful storms from causing so much damage year after year. But as weather experts learn more about how tornadoes develop, life-saving tornado warnings will be quicker and more effective. Someday we may be able to predict tornadoes the way we can predict tomorrow's weather.

CHAPTER NOTES

CHAPTER 1. GREENSBURG IN RUINS

1. Wes Wyatt and Steven Ray, "Greensburg, KS Tornado," *WVUA-TV Weather Blog,* May 7, 2007, <http://sky7weather.wordpress.com/2007/-5/-7/greensburg-ks-tornado/> (August 9, 2007).

2. "Greensburg Kansas Tornado," *Disaster Services International,* May 7, 2007, <http://www.disasterservice.org/latest/greensburg-kansas.html> (August 9, 2007).

3. Ibid; Sarah Shatz, "Tornado Town - Notes from Greensburg, Kansas," *The Digital Journalist,* August 2007,<http://www.digitaljournalist.org/issue0708/tornado-town-notes-from-greensburg-kansas.html> (September 4, 2007).

4. Sarah Shatz.

5. "Survivor Found in Kansas Tornado Rubble," *CBS News,* May 7, 2007, <http://www.cbsnews.com/stories/2007/05/07/national/main2765987.shtml> (August 10, 2007).

6. Associated Press, "Kansas Tornado Death Toll Hits 10," *MSNBC.com,* May 8, 2007, <http://www.msnbc.msn.com/id/18551775/> (August 10, 2007).

CHAPTER 2. WHAT'S THE WEATHER?

1. National Weather Service, Portland, Oregon, "Spotters In ACTION, Winter 2006-2007," *Pacific NW Spotter Newsletter, www.weather.gov/Portland,* April 2007, <http://www.wrh.noaa.gov/pqr/info/pdf/SpotterApr07.pdf> (September 10, 2007).

CHAPTER 3. UNDERSTANDING TORNADOES

1. "Tornadoes," *National Oceanic & Atmospheric Administration (NOAA),* January 16, 2007, <http://www.noaa.gov/tornadoes.html> (September 10, 2007).

CHAPTER 4. WHEN A TORNADO HITS

1. "Tornadoes," *National Oceanic & Atmospheric Administration (NOAA)*, January 16, 2007, <http://www.noaa.gov/tornadoes.html> (September 10, 2007).

2. "Tornado Climatology, National Oceanic and Atmospheric Administration Global Climate Monitoring," *NOAA Satellite and Information Service, National Climatic Data Center*, September 5, 2007, <http://www.ncdc.noaa.gov/oa/climate/severeweather/tornadoes.html> (September 24, 2007).

3. Daniel P. Brown and Joel Rothfuss, "An Approach to Waterspout Forecasting for South Florida and the Keys," *National Weather Service Forecast Office Miami-South Florida*, January 7, 2005, <http://www.srh.noaa.gov/mfl/newpage/research/SPOUT.html> (September 20, 2007).

CHAPTER 5. TRACKING TORNADOES

1. Keli Tarp, "New Radar Technology Can Increase Tornado Warning Lead Times: Navy's Phased Array Radar Being Adapted for Weather Use," *NOAA Celebrates 200 Years of Science, Service, and Stewardship*, July 2, 2007, <http://celebrating200years.noaa.gov/magazine/phased_array_radar/welcome.html> (September 28, 2007).

2. NOAA, National Weather Service, "What Is SKYWARN™?" *National Weather Service SKYWARN™*, November 20, 2007, <http://www.weather.gov/skywarn/> (June 18, 2008).

3. Bijal P. Trivedi, *National Geographic News*, June 27, 2003, <http://news.nationalgeographic.com/news/pf/56024506.html> (June 18, 2008).

GLOSSARY

air masses—Portions of the atmosphere that move around Earth's surface.

air pressure—The weight of the molecules of the atmosphere.

atmosphere—A mixture of gases, including nitrogen, oxygen, carbon dioxide, and water vapor, that surrounds Earth.

condense—Change from a gas, such as water vapor, into a liquid or solid as the temperature is lowered.

cumulonimbus—A type of cloud consisting of a tall tower of dense, mound-shaped clouds with a low, flat bottom. This type of cloud is also called a thunderhead because it produces thunderstorms, with rain, snow, or hail. It may give rise to tornadoes.

cyclone—A hurricane in the Indian Ocean and nearby regions; a term also used to describe a tornado.

debris—The pieces of something that has been destroyed or torn apart.

downdraft—A downward current of air.

evaporate—Change from a liquid to a gas as the temperature is raised.

funnel cloud—A cone-shaped cloud that forms at the bottom of a thunderhead; may develop into a tornado.

hailstones—Tiny balls of ice condensed from water droplets in clouds.

high-pressure system—A weather system of generally sinking air that tends to bring calm, clear weather.

hurricane—A violent tropical storm with circular winds surrounding a low-pressure area of calm air, called the eye.

lightning—A sudden release of electricity within or from a storm cloud, producing a brilliant flash of light.

low-pressure system—A weather system in which rising air currents form clouds and tend to bring unstable, stormy weather.

meteorologist—A scientist who studies weather.

molecules—Microscopic particles that make up matter.

precipitation—Condensation of water vapor in the atmosphere so that it falls to Earth's surface in the form of rain, snow, or hail.

storm chaser—Someone who keeps track of weather reports and travels to places where tornadoes have been reported.

storm spotter—A volunteer who belongs to SKYWARN™, an organization created by the National Weather Service, and is specially trained to report local severe weather conditions, including tornadoes.

supercell—A type of thunderstorm that rotates and is most likely to give birth to strong or long-lived tornadoes.

thunder—The sound produced by the explosion of air molecules heated by a bolt of lightning.

tornado—An extremely violent storm in the form of a funnel of spinning air.

Tornado Alley—The region in the central part of the United States, where tornadoes are most common.

tornado outbreak—A group of six or more tornadoes occurring in the same region around the same time.

updraft—An upward current of air.

vortex—A spinning column of air that draws everything to its center.

water cycle—The processes of evaporation, condensation, and precipitation that keep water circulating between Earth's surface and the atmosphere.

water vapor—Water in the gas state, formed by the evaporation of the liquid.

waterspout—A tornado that forms over oceans, seas, or lakes.

weather forecaster—A person who uses information on current weather conditions, such as atmospheric pressure, temperature, wind speed and direction, precipitation, humidity, and cloud formation, supplemented by computer analyses, to predict future weather conditions.

wind shear—A change in wind speed or direction over short distances.

FURTHER READING

Challoner, Jack. *Hurricane & Tornado*. New York: DK Publishing, Inc., 2004.

Nicolson, Cynthia Pratt. *Tornado!* Tonawanda, N.Y.: Kids Can Press Ltd., 2003.

Reed, Jim. *Storm Chaser: A Photographer's Journey*. New York: Harry N. Abrams Books, 2007.

Scavuzzo, Wendy. *Tornado Alert!* New York: Crabtree Publishing Company, 2004.

Spilsbury, Richard, and Louise Spilsbury. *Hurricanes and Tornadoes (Natural Disasters)*. London: Hodder Wayland, 2007.

Woods, Michael, and Mary Woods. *Tornadoes*. Minneapolis, Minn.: Lerner Publications Company, 2007.

INTERNET ADDRESSES

Weather: What Forces Affect Our Weather: Storm Chaser
<http://www.learner.org/interactives/weather/act_tornado/>
Interactive site based on programs from Planet Earth: Using photos, maps, and a Storm Spotter's Guidebook, check the weather in Kansas cities and compare your predictions to those of experts.

Weather Wiz Kids: Tornadoes
<http://www.weatherwizkids.com/tornado.htm>
Indiana meteorologist Crystal Wicker gives information about tornadoes and other weather; with games, experiments, photos, jokes, folklore, and flashcards. E-mail weather questions to Crystal.

Owlie Skywarn's Weather Book: Watch Out . . .Tornadoes
<http://www.nws.noaa.gov/om/brochures/owlie-tornado.pdf>
NOAA brochure for kids with information about tornadoes and a quiz.

INDEX